EDDIE KAT

# Nobody's
# CHILDREN

### A Fostering Journey through Heartbreak and Healing

Unless otherwise indicated, all scripture quotations are taken from the Holy Bible, New Living Translation, Copyright © 1996, 2004, 2015 by Tyndale House Foundation. Used by permission of Tyndale House Publishers, Inc., Carol Stream, Illinois 60188. All rights reserved. Scripture quotations marked (KJV) taken from the Holy Bible, King James Version, which is in the public domain. Scripture quotations marked (NIV) are taken from the Holy Bible, New International Version®, NIV®. Copyright © 1973, 1978, 1984, 2011 by Biblica, Inc.™ Used by permission of Zondervan. All rights reserved worldwide. www.zondervan.com The "NIV" and "New International Version" are trademarks registered in the United States Patent and Trademark Office by Biblica, Inc.™ Scripture quotations are from the ESV® Bible (The Holy Bible, English Standard Version®), © 2001 by Crossway, a publishing ministry of Good News Publishers. Used by permission. All rights reserved. The ESV text may not be quoted in any publication made available to the public by a Creative Commons license. The ESV may not be translated in whole or in part into any other language.

Soft cover ISBN: 978-1-4866-2607-6
eBook ISBN: 978-1-4866-2608-3

Word Alive Press
119 De Baets Street Winnipeg, MB  R2J 3R9
www.wordalivepress.ca

**WORD ALIVE**
—P R E S S—

Cataloguing in Publication information can be obtained from Library and Archives Canada.

This book contains descriptions of childhood sexual assault, addiction, and trauma. It addresses themes that may be distressing to some readers, including accounts of physical and emotional abuse, manipulation, and their long-term psychological impacts. Take care when reading. If you find the content overwhelming, consider seeking support from a trusted individual or professional.

Pure and genuine religion in the sight of God the Father means caring for orphans and widows in their distress and refusing to let the world corrupt you. (James 1:27)

My sacrifice, O God, is a broken spirit; a broken and contrite heart you, God, will not despise. (Psalm 51:17, NIV)

The Lord is near to the brokenhearted and saves the crushed in spirit. Many are the afflictions of the righteous, but the Lord delivers him out of them all. (Psalm 34:18–19, ESV)

# Contents

# Preface

THIS BOOK IS based on factual events which took place in our family. My wife and I have been born-again Christians for thirty years now. My wife and I met when we were both nineteen years old in 1989. I had moved up from the east coast to work for the Hudson's Bay Company. A year later, we were married. We'll be celebrating thirty-four years of marriage this coming September.

After we married, we quickly found out we were unable to conceive. Since we both loved children, we decided to become foster parents. We fostered two beautiful children in the early 1990s and wanted to adopt them but met roadblocks with the child welfare agency. After all, they were Indigenous children and I was white. Even though my wife was Indigenous, they wouldn't allow us to adopt. Feeling crushed, we walked away from the pain of fostering.

However, ten years later we decided to foster again. We fostered for twelve more years… and a lot happened in those twelve years.

We adopted two children and fostered more than forty others. Among them were three children from the same family. These were special needs children and required a lot of love and attention. Nevertheless, we began the process of adopting them.

Because of a long history of sexual abuse and incest in this family, the children had suffered damage. As they grew older and became teenagers, these issues became more prevalent, worrisome, and extreme.

Along the way, God blessed us with a pair of miracles: two babies of our very own.

But little did we know how extreme our foster children's sexual tendencies were. It got to the point where the three siblings began to act out on each other. Not only that, but they became predators to our flesh-and-blood children, who were just two and a half and a newborn at the time.

EVEN AS WE write this book, our hearts are broken over the events that have taken place. We've had our trials and hardships in our walk with God. Miscarrying our first child several years ago was very difficult, but God spoke His word to us, bringing healing and comfort in our time of need.

The pain we now experience has been so overwhelming that our hearts ache. We have a constant lump in our throats and sudden urges to break out in tears.

Just today, my wife spoke a word of encouragement to me about the battle we face. She told me that she'd been pondering how God gave us His best, Jesus, and how God our Father always has the best in mind for us. He is always willing to pour out His blessings on mankind.

However, although God gives us anything we could possibly think of or ask for, we often reject him. As a matter of fact, billions of people reject God every day, even well-meaning Christians who at times turn their backs on God even after all He has done for us.

So why should it be different for us?

We have provided everything for our children—financially, academically, athletically, and socially. We've taken trips from one end of Canada to the other, seeing every beautiful province, trying every amusement park ride, riding every water slide, and enjoying every kind of excitement a kid could dream of.

Yet they in turn stole from us, lied, betrayed our trust, and perpetrated unimaginable acts on those who loved them most dearly.

"How could they?" one might wonder.

Well, God is the only one who knows and feels our rejection. As 2 Corinthians 1:3–5 declares,

> Praise be to the God and Father of our Lord Jesus Christ, the Father of compassion and the God of all comfort, who comforts us in all our troubles, so that we can comfort those in any trouble with the comfort we ourselves receive from God. For just as we share abundantly in the sufferings of Christ, so also our comfort abounds through Christ.

Wow! You see, God comforts us so we can comfort others.

We have been Christians for thirty years and faithfully served Him through ministering His word, leading people into the presence of God through song, pastoring youth, intern pastoring, directing boys and girls clubs, and sitting on church boards. We have been faithful in every aspect of our Christian walk, yet horrendous tragedies have still taken place in our home. Why?

It's all so we can draw near to God and He can draw near to us. He comforts us so we can comfort others. Jesus walked this earth and was tested in every way we are tested, through lust of the flesh, lust of the eyes, and pride of life. He was tempted in every area yet remained sinless. He was God incarnate, God as one of us, God in the flesh—but with supernatural powers! No, he wasn't Superman. He was a man like you and me. We are human.

Many born-again believers feel that they need to live perfect lives. Not at all. Only one person was ever perfect, and He was crucified!

We therefore turn to that age-old question: why do bad things happen to good people? The answer, from my perspective, is that God wants to draw near to us, comforting us so we can comfort others. We face challenges so He can be glorified.

Our story, as tragic and horrific as it may sound right now, will bring glory to God, and from it God will bring healing.

# 1

## Nobody's Children

PICTURE THIS: A boy of twelve, unkept, with scraggly hair, dirty face, and torn clothes. He isn't dressed for the elements. At a time of the year when kids should be getting settled into school, making new friends, and feeling out their new teacher to see how far they can push the limits, this boy wanders the streets aimlessly. He gets escorted out of stores during school hours and sent on his way. It's early in the school year and he isn't even registered for classes. Shame on his parents! Don't they care? What's their problem? Someone should report them for neglect...

Actually, the boy I just described is a child in care. His parents have already lost their rights to him. The child welfare agency has taken over.

Yet what has just been described sure sounds like neglect, correct? Yes. This boy is neglected and left to fend for himself, despite living at a receiving home.

For those who may be unaware, a receiving home is a house for children who are waiting for placement in foster care. Perhaps there are no foster homes available, or perhaps they have issues that make it difficult to place them. Hopefully they're only in the receiving home temporarily, but sadly many remain in receiving homes for years.

This boy is under the protection of the agency, yet he is still neglected, uncared for, and unregistered to receive an education. How can this be? Isn't the point of a child being taken into the foster system to care for them? That's the idea.

Are children who are taken out of their homes because of problems in the family more neglected at home or in the care of an agency?

When my wife Annie saw this boy, she immediately called the agency for some answers. She wanted to find out why this boy wasn't in school. The answer she was given was that they didn't have all the paperwork—birth certificate, immunization records, etc.—to register him. She then asked why the boy was allowed to wander the streets.

It turned out that this boy had already been at the receiving home for three to four weeks. He was nobody's child. Whether at home or in care, he was abandoned, left to raise himself.

This book is meant to open our eyes to the harsh reality of the child welfare system. It's broken, and a broken system produces broken children, broken families, and broken lives. The system is supposed to be a resource for families when they need help. It's supposed to bring healing and restoration, assisting and strengthening families, yet it produces only pain and separation. It destroys people and demoralizes all who walk through its doors.

When Annie and I think of agency, our blood pressure rises and we feel physically ill. We know the majority of frontline workers are not to blame for the loss and hurt inflicted on children and their families. A lot of it has to do with the decision-making of upper management.

Yet that would be a whole other book. Within these pages, we want to share our experiences—to enlighten you and bring you to your knees in order to pray for these families caught in the revolving door of agency.

# 2

## The Fam Jam

AFTER ELEVEN YEARS of marriage, Annie and I still hadn't conceived our own child, so we agreed to open our home to foster children. We were interviewed and submitted to a house assessment to ensure we would be a safe home.

Initially we thought it would take some time to receive our first foster child, but we were naive and unaware of the great need. We had informed the agency that we were willing to serve as an "emergency home," which meant sometimes taking children short-term for a period of days, weeks, or perhaps months. We had fostered for a short stint back in the early 1990s in another province, but we hadn't dealt with this agency and didn't know what we were getting ourselves into.

From day one, we should have known things weren't as they seemed. Taking in teenagers hadn't been on our list. As we had informed the agency, we were only interested in kids between the ages of four and twelve. The first two foster children we kept? You guessed it: two teenagers! One of them was okay, but the other was very oppositional and had a lot of issues!

So we reminded the agency that we didn't want to take in teenagers.

Over the course of about two years, forty children came and went through our house. As one could imagine, it was difficult when children stayed for short durations only to leave as soon as we began to get attached. We then told the agency we wanted to be more of a long-term foster home for children who wouldn't be going home for quite some time, or maybe even not at all.

Our family developed over the next few years.

Jimmy came into our care, and three years later his sister Ericka came to join us. We adopted them after a lengthy process. Their biological parents sped up the process by signing their parental rights over to us through the courts. That might sound cold, but it's one of the greatest acts of love Annie and I had ever seen. Those parents knew that their children were in a good home and that we would love and care for them like they were our own. What a selfless act!

We never denied the parents access to their kids. When they were in town, we allowed them to go out for dinner dates with Jimmy and Ericka. We even had the parents over for Easter and Christmas. The only stipulation was that we didn't want the parents to come around if they were under the influence of alcohol. They never did.

We had a good working relationship with those parents and thanked them for allowing us to raise their beautiful children!

Then there was Nate and Johnny. We were only supposed to have these boys for several months, after which they were to be reintegrated with their biological father, who had started a new life in a different community.

To make a long story short—for now anyway—there was a breakdown in the reintegration process and the boys needed to stay with us long term. All six siblings in that family had gotten together for a family visit. Something happened at that visit, but all we were told was that the children would never go back to living with their father.

We should have requested more information, but we just took this at face value.

Three years after Nate and Johnny came to live with us, we decided to take their baby sister Angel. She had been in a receiving home, just like her brothers before her. What caught my wife's attention was the fact that this one-year-old had been bounced around between three local receiving homes in a few short months. That bothered us. Every child needs stability.

So when Annie asked me whether we could take her in, naturally I said yes.

Just like that, we had five children: two adopted and three in care.

We had been married nineteen years and come to terms with the fact that we wouldn't have any of our own biological children. We told the Lord, "We'll be happy with the five little blessings You've already given us. We'll do the best we can to raise them in Your love and admonition."

About a month or two later, we found out we were pregnant! Isn't that the way it always is? You come to terms with it not happening and then you finally get pregnant.

My wife had always said that she wanted to have a baby before she was forty. God has a sense of humour, you know; we found out we were pregnant on April 1 and our first daughter was born three weeks before our fortieth birthdays!

If you're keeping count, that means we were up to six children. Good thing we had bought that eight-seater SUV a few years earlier.

We might have thought that was it, right? When you wait nineteen years to give birth to your first child, what are the chances you'll have another?

Pretty good, it turned out. At forty-two years of age, we had Josie, another beautiful girl.

That made seven kids—Jimmy (fifteen), Nate (fourteen), Johnny (thirteen), Ericka (twelve), Angel (seven), Jewels (two), and Josie (three months). There you have it: the Kat family!

# 3

## Set Up to Fail

THE SUV JUST didn't do it for us anymore. We had to go bigger!

Shortly after Josie's birth, we took a trip to the big city. While there, I laid eyes on a beautiful fifteen-passenger van. The van was solid, with a little rust on the undercarriage. But it was a price we could afford. With seven children, affordable is always a good price! So we purchased the van and went on our merry way.

A few short weeks later, the air conditioner stopped working, so I took it to the shop. To my surprise, the garage informed me that the tires were in rough shape and needed replacing. I don't know much about tires, but when the mechanic showed me the steel wires popping through the threads, I figured it was a pretty good sign it was time to swap them out. I footed the bill for four brand-new tires.

If it hadn't been for the air conditioner, we would have never known about the tires. Most likely, we would have had a blowout on one of our many journeys. It would have led to a horrific accident.

We had been set up to fail. Whether it was intentional, an oversight, or just plain cheapness on the part of the dealer, the result could have been tragic.

Have you ever been assigned to complete a task but not given the right tools or information needed to get it done properly? When you start a new job, your new employers don't just bring you on board, sit you down at a desk, and expect you to jump in. No. They give you an orientation, introduce you to the team, go through your job description, and let you know what's expected of you. They'll also give you the tools, passwords, and resources to do the job. If they don't, you're being set up to fail.

This describes the foster care system. We had fostered twice in two separate communities. When we began fostering the second time, the system had twenty-four foster homes. After eleven years of fostering in that community, there remained only four homes. Why did this happen? Was it just that people didn't care about fostering anymore?

No, not at all.

The agency didn't seem to understand why they had lost so many foster homes, but here is the reason: foster parents are treated like dirt. The system says that it will be there to provide support and assistance when a foster home needs it, whether it's relief, respite, reimbursement, counselling, or providing one-on-one support workers. They say that they'll provide whatever you need.

But there's a big difference between telling people what you'll do for them and actually doing those things.

As foster parents, we sometimes felt looked down upon by many workers with the agency. We heard workers make remarks like "They're just in it for the money" or "Well, now that they had their own child, they'll probably give up their foster kids."

Also, the financial assistance we received for fostering didn't cover all our needs. Let me put it this way: before we had kids, we had lots of money and no bills. Afterward we had lots of bills and no money!

Countless times, we asked the agency whether we would be reimbursed for spending money on the kids. For example, we purchased a set of secondhand goalie equipment for one of the boys. The cost was about $1,000. Would we be reimbursed, we asked?

"Oh yeah! Go ahead. Just get a receipt and we'll pay you back."

Awesome!

But it was a different story when it came time to collect. Then they told us, "Oh, well, that had to be approved by my supervisor. Anyway, there's not enough money allocated for that type of purchase!" We were out thousands of dollars because we were never reimbursed.

After a while, we didn't even bother to submit receipts for the extra money we spent on the kids. We knew the agency was going to fight us anyway.

Their policy binder stated that respite was an option, and they actually encouraged foster parents to take regular relief when needed. However, when parents asked for the relief, they were made to feel bad even though it was their right. And if the agency did provide relief, it only happened at their convenience.

We once asked for relief when I was attending a conference and my wife wanted to go away for a girls weekend. We told the agency when we wanted the boys picked up and dropped off.

So what did the workers do? They picked them up a day early and dropped them off the next day. In so doing this, the boys missed out on a major exam at school, a class party, a special cadet ceremony, a Halloween event night held at the local church, and a hockey game. The dates we had provided were an inconvenience to the agency workers.

An inconvenience? If it doesn't line up with the workers' agenda, that's too bad.

Countless times, workers have called us up and told us they were coming by to meet with us or the kids. "Whatever day and time works for you is good," they would say. But when we would suggest a day and time, their response was often the same: "It's not good for us."

Nate's counselling sessions were held during school hours, meaning he had to miss close to three hours of school every time. That was the best time for the counsellor. The driver would pick him up from school and take him to his session, where he'd wait. After the session, he'd wait again to be brought back to school, almost three hours later.

One time, the driver dropped him off for his session but then informed him that she wouldn't be able to bring him back after. He would have to find his own way home. Not even his counsellor helped him get a ride. So he sat in the front waiting area until he finally thought to see whether I could come get him. I had to leave work and pick him up even though it was the agency's responsibility.

Nate, Johnny, and Angel were all special needs. They'd had numerous psychological assessments and tests to diagnose them with fetal alcohol syndrome/fetal alcohol effects (FAS/FAE), attention deficit hyperactivity disorder (ADHD), and even possibly obsessive-compulsive disorder (OCD). When a child receives a diagnosis, the foster parents are to receive a special rate. But after nine years of having the two boys in our care, we still only received a special rate for one of them—and that only happened for the last two years. We had Angel for six years and didn't receive a special rate for her, either.

Now, you may be wondering, "I thought you said it wasn't about the money!" It's not. But if we're eligible for a rate, we should be getting the rate. We spent a lot more money than we received from the agency in per diem rates.

Johnny, the more hyperactive of the two brothers, loved taking things apart to see how they worked. When he got mad at us, he would sometimes break things to get back at us. One time I went to a Toronto Raptors game and bought souvenirs for all the kids. I bought Johnny a foam Raptors head. He loved it!

But a day later, he got mad at me for not allowing him to play video games. It just wasn't the right time for video games, since we usually kept that privilege for weekends. To get back at me, he went downstairs and ripped up the foam Raptors head.

One Christmas, he got mad because I told him he couldn't yet open one of his gifts. We only let the kids open two gifts per day during the holidays, so they wouldn't get bored right away after playing with every single toy on the first day. Well, he didn't like that.

That night, Jimmy told me that his Xbox wasn't working. Our cable wasn't working downstairs either and the internet was down.

I figured out the problem. Johnny had decided he didn't like being told no, so he'd found a pair of scissors and decided to cut a cable downstairs that led through his bedroom. Later he must have felt bad, because he used scotch tape to put the cable back together.

I could go on and on about the broken doors, seatbelts, toys, furniture, and electronics we had to deal with over the years, literally thousands of dollars of damage and unrepairable merchandise that the agency wouldn't reimburse us for. That's why we kept asking for the special needs rate: to cover all the hidden costs we incurred.

At one point, after fighting with the agency for eight months, they finally found the funds to hire a personal support worker for Nate, Johnny, and Angel. We were relieved. The worker began by taking all three for a period of time, or maybe just two of them. But after a while, we realized that these siblings were playing off each other and it seemed too much for the worker to handle. Soon she only took one at a time.

Here's how that worked out. She was scheduled for forty hours a week at $22 per hour. Pretty good money! After the first month of working with the kids, she submitted her hours to the agency. They wouldn't release her paycheque until she provided a breakdown of what she had done with each kid. This happened several times. It got to the point where the worker had to take a second job in order to make ends meet!

She only lasted four months, providing some respite here and there when she could because her other job took her away from us.

We didn't blame her, as she had bills to pay. We blame the agency for giving her a hard time over her hours, many times withholding pay, and in so doing forcing her to go elsewhere.

We were set up to fail!

The way the agency deals with foster parents makes no sense at all. They don't want to give parents the special needs rate. And they give their support workers such a hard time that they quit.

And yet we've heard that they take children into care in the north and send them to the far south of the province where homes receive anywhere from $100 to $300 per day per child! We know this for a fact because we were told so by various workers in the system.

All we asked for was a special rate of $75 a day.

We know of one child who has two workers living twenty-four hours a day in their own house. That's one child with two workers, costing $100–300 per day. Do the math. What does it cost to pay two workers on a monthly basis? It could be anywhere from $6,000 to $18,000.

So the agency is willing to ship children from their homes in the north, where their families and cultural roots are, to the far south, an eight- to ten-hour drive, where they have no roots, no friends, and no connections. And they're willing to pay great amounts of money to do it, all while refusing to provide a family like ours a measly $75 bucks per day.

Come on! There's something wrong with this system.

It all comes down to passing the buck. It's easier to pass the buck than to deal with foster parents and provide services, supports, resources, and assistance when needed. For many workers with the agency, it's a real nice pay cheque. The workers who have a heart for children in care and families in crisis usually don't last long, though, because they burn out. They care too much.

Is it any wonder that a community like ours could go from twenty-four foster homes to only four in eleven years? We felt unsupported as foster parents, left on our own to deal with issues as they arose. Only when a home was on the verge of closing its doors would the agency step in, but by then it was often too late.

For us, it was almost too late. We didn't close our home, but there was a great deal of damage done.

## Help!

> In my distress I called to the Lord; I cried to
> my God for help. From his temple he heard my
> voice; my cry came before him, into his ears.
> (Psalm 18:6)

WHEN ALL ELSE fails, we can call on God. He will always hear our cry for help.

You've probably heard the following scenario posed many times. What if you were walking along the street and saw a house burning and knew there were people inside? Wouldn't you call for help? Wouldn't you call out for them or run in to offer assistance before it was too late?

Of course, any decent person would do what's right. They would help!

But what if you were the ones inside the burning house and you were calling out for help and no one came? What if, through the flames, you saw people walk by, look your way, then keep walking on by?

It's frustrating when you request help, knowing there are resources to help you out, but no one takes you seriously. People just think you're overreacting, blowing things out of proportion.

They basically don't think you know what you're talking about. They think you're being silly.

This has been our journey and track record with the child welfare agency.

In the previous chapter, I talked about foster parents being set up to fail. When a child comes into your care, you receive only minimal information. Next to nothing. When we were serving as an emergency home, workers would show up with a child who had just been apprehended, then give us a checklist of some basic background information, including likes, habits, routines, and favourite foods. More often than not, these factsheets were useless. We had to find out about these kids on our own and then question the agency concerning our findings. They would feign ignorance: "Oh, we didn't know!" And when we'd ask for assistance, they say, "Well, good luck with that!"

When Nate was ten, he received a laptop through school to help him with his academic studies from elementary to university and beyond, wherever his educational path took him. This assistive technology was made accessible due to his diagnosis.

Well, Jimmy's older brother came to stay with us for the Christmas holidays. Jimmy, his brother, and Nate watched some movies one night, and afterward, when everyone was in bed, Jimmy's older brother introduced Nate to pornography. This was the beginning of a very slippery slope.

Shortly after this happened, Nate's conscience got the best of him and he told us all about it. Annie explained that she was proud of him for coming clean and that he shouldn't access it again.

There are two things we didn't tolerate in our household: stealing and lying. We always told our kids to tell the truth, no matter what, even if it meant getting into trouble. The consequences aren't as harsh when a child is honest.

At the time, we didn't report the incident to the agency. We thought it was an isolated incident.

But a year later, we found out that Nate had again accessed porn, and this time it was more severe. He lost his computer privileges, was grounded, and missed out on a motocross event during the March break.

We then reported the porn use to the agency, although they dismissed it as a regular part of growing up, something that's natural for teenagers to explore. We asked them for counselling. After asking for it repeatedly, Nate received a forty-five-minute weekly session held at school. The counselling consisted of playing board games and talking about his feelings. What a joke!

We were getting ready to move to a new town, mainly for educational reasons. We wanted our children to be better prepared for high school.

While getting ready for a major yard sale, we found out that Nate had torn a hole in the end of his bedspring to hide his video games. We had suspected something was going on, since he was very tired some days.

After a little more investigating, we realized that he had also used his game console to access a vast amount of porn. We were not impressed.

Again, the agency blew us off by saying this was a part of growing up.

Once we had moved, we had to work with a second agency which acted as a middleman. Perhaps having a new agency would mean more assistance and resources, right? No. It was the same old broken system.

We once discovered that Nate had taken some of our girls' underwear and hidden it in his bed. He denied it at first, of course, but we knew when our kids were lying and eventually got the truth.

When we told his new counsellor of this newfound fetish, the advice she gave us was to buy Nate his own special girls panties and a special towel for him to masturbate with.

Let me ask you this: would you buy an alcoholic liquor? How about a drug addict? Would it be wise to bring someone addicted to gambling to a casino? No! So why would you support and encourage that type of behaviour?

"Absolutely not," my wife told the counsellor. "That's a ludicrous idea."

We later told this story to other counsellors and police officers we knew, and everyone agreed that this didn't make any sense. In fact, they were dumbfounded that we would be offered this advice.

On another occasion, I found Nate and Johnny in Nate's bed one Saturday morning. At the time, they said that they were tickling each other. The agency dismissed it as roughhousing.

We eventually enrolled the kids in a private school with an excellent student-to-teacher ratio. With students on every side of him, Nate still took every opportunity to access porn at school. He got caught twice in one year and ended up not attending the senior school trip. He also asked a girl three years younger if she wanted to kiss him. When we found out about this, we informed the school staff and the agency. The agency, of course, just thought it was harmless.

This went on for about four years and we became very alarmed. We even told Nate point-blank: "If you don't stop accessing porn, it will eat you up and destrcy you. Viewing porn isn't harmless. It's not a victimless crime. When people watch it, they need more and more to satisfy the urge. They turn to more warped videos, maybe even child porn. When that's not enough, they begin to act out on it, usually on the helpless."

We were very concerned.

One December, we told the agency, "Look, we feel Nate needs some intervention." We wanted some intensive counselling for him. Maybe he could even attend a treatment centre. And when my wife made this suggestion, our workers laughed at her.

"Pornography is normal at that age," they said. "You can't get treatment, and you don't need treatment, for porn. That's ridiculous!"

But they humoured us and set up some counselling sessions for Nate, which took place six months later.

Around April, we arranged for Nate, Johnny, and Angel to undergo some full assessments with a well-known psychologist to determine how well they were developing. This of course had required many phone calls and requests put in to the agency.

When the appointments finally came, I was unable to take them, since I couldn't take the time off. My wife was finishing a four-month college course and also couldn't take them. So I suggested that their support worker could take them. After all, it was their job to take care of these sorts of appointments. Although of course either me or Annie would have gone if we could have.

As soon as the kids left town for these appointments down south, my wife began to beat herself up. But if she had taken the time to make the trip, she would have failed her course and thrown three months of college down the tubes.

We were informed the boys would have a male chaperone to stay with them in one hotel room while the usual female worker would stay in a separate room with Angel. It sounded okay to us.

Upon their return from the four-day trip, after the workers dropped off the kids and immediately left, Angel took Annie aside and told her that Johnny had asked her to kiss him during their visit.

Johnny was twelve and Angel was six.

"What visit?" we asked.

As far as we knew, no visits other than the appointments with the psychologist had been arranged for this trip.

That's when the kids told us that the agency workers had dropped them off on Friday afternoon to see their two older siblings, aged fifteen and sixteen, on their way back. It had been an overnight visit.

We were livid! Whenever they visited their family members, problems were sure to follow.

We immediately called the support worker on her cell and told her to get back to our house. Upon her arrival, we asked about the unscheduled sibling visit and why it had taken place.

"My supervisor knew about this and approved it," she said.

We had another question, based on the conversation we'd just had with the kids. "And why were all five siblings allowed to sleep in the same room when there was only one set of bunkbeds?"

The worker explained that the older siblings, Gerry and Josiah, were living in an approved foster home. There had been two rooms, and everything had been arranged so it would be appropriate.

But the children had all snuck into the same bedroom, we learned. They'd stayed up all night laughing, joking, and fooling around. Josiah had taken the top bunk, with Nate and his sister Gerry on the bottom bunk. Johnny and Angel had lain on the floor.

They didn't "sleep," though.

When our worker asked Johnny about what happened, he was honest: "Yeah, I asked Angel to kiss me."

Now, if the agency had done their job properly, they would have performed a full investigation to find out what happened. But in our experience, we felt they very rarely did their jobs to the best of their ability, or in the best interest of the children.

All they did was call the foster home where all five children had stayed overnight.

At that point, we told the agency that we wanted Johnny removed from our home. What had happened was far too inappropriate. All our trust was broken. For him to try that with his own sister was sick and twisted.

They didn't take him back, of course, because they didn't have anywhere else to place him. However, they worked to get a support worker to spend several hours with Johnny per week, so we could get some respite.

This solution was very short-term and didn't last long.

I noticed something else very strange about Johnny, Nate, and Angel after this unscheduled visit with their older siblings. They suddenly wanted to call their siblings to talk to them. I heard Nate crying while on the phone with Gerry, telling her that he missed her. This struck me as very odd since they only saw each other once a year and he never cried!

It didn't sit well with me. Something was up. I had my suspicions, but I couldn't say for sure.

We made a big stink about the whole situation, and about a month later both of the welfare agencies we dealt with wanted to meet with us to review the report from the specialist. We came to the table expecting to hear the results of the psychological assessments and receive some guidance as to helping the children be successful in school and at home.

What we got was a punch to the gut.

The report declared that the children would be better off being sent to a different foster home in a different region. There they would receive more resources. The boys would stay in one foster home while Angel would live in another close by. The three siblings would still see each other on a regular basis.

Quite frankly, we were very taken aback. We had been expecting to receive some new resources and tools, but instead they wanted to rip these children from our home—in just one week's time.

"How will you break it to the children?" they asked.

Shocked and dumbfounded, we needed to take a few moments to regain our composure. Then we dug in our heels and fought back.

"We asked for help," I said. "We asked for psychological tests to learn the severity of the damage they suffered during pregnancy due to their biological mother's drinking. Our intention was never to give up! Sure, we're sometimes frustrated by their behaviours. But giving up isn't really an option for us. We loved them too much."

Rather than walk away and let the agency close our home, a righteous anger rose up in us.

"What if we fight for them?" Annie asked.

"Then we'll have to go back to our supervisors and see what our options are," one of the workers told us.

Why had they suddenly decided to try and remove the children? Was it to cover something up? Was it because certain people in the agency had gotten into some trouble over the mess of that unscheduled visit?

This we know for sure: the decision wasn't being made in the children's best interests. Personally, I think someone had a personal vendetta against us, all because we had always stood up for the rights of the children.

We decided to seek more help—from medical professionals, from support workers specializing in FAS, from counsellors, and even from lawyers. I'm very thankful for everyone who did what they could to help us keep the children.

When I spoke to our regular support worker, I told her that I didn't know how much we should talk about the ongoing situation, since we were in the process of retaining a lawyer. She informed me that anything I said would be recorded. Considering that, I had nothing else to say.

We met again a few weeks later to discuss the future of the children. Now the agency backed up, having opted to allow the children to remain in our care. Once they saw how dedicated we were, they must have known they were in for a messy fight.

I think they also knew they were in the wrong.

During the follow-up meeting, though, they stated that they wanted to provide a personal support worker for the three children. That was all we had ever wanted.

Well, it took eight months for that personal support worker to start coming around. In the meantime, the agencies kept passing the buck.

After this scare, the agency agreed to start counselling for Nate. It was provided only inconsistently at first and seemed pointless. The school year ended and another began, and through it all Nate kept right on accessing porn from his school laptop. This third infraction in two years resulted in a suspension.

Once again, we went to the agency and told them that Nate needed more intense counselling. They agreed to increase the sessions to several times a week.

But nothing changed in the six weeks to follow. It didn't matter what we did. When we took Nate's laptop away, he used his gaming console. He also used computers at school, loading up videos on memory sticks to be viewed later whenever he could. He snuck onto other computers, and at one point he even convinced his brother at school to visit porn sites.

It doesn't matter what safeguards you have, what kind of firewalls you put up; an addict will do whatever he needs to get his fix.

**5**

## The Summer of Pain

AH, THE SUMMER solstice! June 21 is a time of excitement, planning, and looking forward to summer vacation. It's also a time to get things done you couldn't get done the rest of the year.

For me, as a schoolteacher, it's a joyous time because it means I get two months off! I enjoy my summers tremendously and we always do so much with our children. We love to travel, go to fairs, and hit the open road and the beach. That summer, I planned to do some gardening, renovations, and minor repairs around the house.

Instead that summer went down in history as a very painful time in our lives.

Everything started to unravel earlier in the month. Nate's Grade Eight graduation happened on a Thursday evening, June 7. It was a moving and touching time. Although we had gone through a lot with him in the last few years, this night was special. We had seen him work through much adversity to get to this point.

As part of my job, I always prepared a PowerPoint presentation about the eighth-grade graduates. A lot of time, effort, and preparation went into this ten-minute presentation. I wanted their parents to be touched by seeing the growth of their children.

Nate's graduation, including his speech and receiving his diploma, was a momentous occasion for us. Annie later said that when Nate finished his speech, she wanted to run up to the front and give him a big hug! I told her she should have; there wouldn't have been a dry eye in the house!

Yes, we were very proud of Nate.

Two days later, though, on Saturday morning, things weren't as peachy. I got up early as usual with baby Josie, and Jewels usually got up early too. Nate and Johnny were then the next to wake up, on a typical Saturday. I always told them to sleep in, because it was the only day they could.

When Nate still hadn't gotten up by 9:00 a.m., I woke him up. He was very tired, but I let it go. I gave him and his brother their medication, since Nate had ADD and Johnny ADHD. It took Johnny a little while to settle down before the meds kicked in, so I told him to stay in bed for a bit longer. When Johnny eventually got up, I had him eat.

Then the boys started doing their chores. After all, everyone in our house did chores. Everyone pulled their own weight. We were training our children for the time when they'd move out on their own to attend college or university. We wanted them to have some life skills.

Nate's chore that morning was to take the load of laundry out of the dryer and then start another load. This is something he did on a regular basis.

Later, closer to lunchtime, Annie asked him to throw on some fries and chicken nuggets. This is also something the older kids had all done many times.

But today was different. Nate was so spaced out.

Now let me explain: whenever he accessed porn, he got this "zombie" look… a very faraway, very spaced-out look. It was almost like he was watching a movie in his head, replaying it repeatedly. We had talked to him about this many times and he admitted that this is exactly what he was doing—revisiting the pornographic images in his mind.

This Saturday morning was bad, worse than normal. The simple task of throwing on some fries and nuggets should have taken a couple of minutes. Today it was a very difficult job for him.

We confronted him about his "zombieness" and asked where he'd been accessing porn this time. He gave us his standard answer: "I'm not accessing it." But we knew our kids. We'd had him for nine years and could tell when something was up.

When the boys' personal support worker came over, we told her to take Nate outside to talk to him about what was going on. He told her that he was stressed out since we were always making him do too many chores. He also accused me of waking him up early when he was tired.

The worker came back inside with Nate, wanting him to tell us what he had told her. He was reluctant at first, probably because it was all lies. The scene was very strange. He sat on the couch with his knees up in his chest, rocking back and forth. We had never seen him do that before. Even the worker hadn't seen behaviour like this.

This worker had previously worked with children who were abused, problematic, and in trouble with the law. She told Nate that he was acting like a victim and should stop it.

He then repeated what he had told the worker, about being stressed out, given too many chores, and waking up early. It was all a crock.

"Well, if you're tired, go lay down," Annie told him.

So Nate went to his room, but he didn't lie down to rest. He just played with his toys. Meanwhile, the support worker took Johnny out in the afternoon for some respite, as she sometimes did on the weekends.

While they were out, Angel went on her tablet, which we had bought for her the previous Christmas. Right away, a picture of porn popped up. Fortunately, her older sister Ericka was there to grab the tablet from her before Angel could tell what it was.

Ericka brought the tablet to us and I checked the date the tablet had been accessed. Sure enough, it had been used two mornings ago. This brought me back to the previous Thursday morning when I'd plugged it in. While watching cartoons with Jewels as usual, I had noticed that Nate wasn't doing the laundry.

"Nate?" I called.

"I'm in the sunroom," he called back.

"Well, get to your chores."

I didn't press the issue, but now it became obvious to me that he had been using Angel's tablet to access porn.

We called the worker and asked her to come back with Johnny. We wanted her there as a witness; we had confronted Nate about viewing porn countless times but rarely had a witness.

When she returned and we talked to him, he knew that he was busted. Once again we reminded him that we knew him and had been able to tell he was up to no good—and now the support worker was able to see through his act. In situations like these, he had used tears, but when we caught on to that tactic he had never tried using tears again. But he did sometimes try it on the worker. She didn't buy into it, though.

We finally had someone on our side who realized that Nate had a problem with porn.

A few days later, on Tuesday, a different worker came over to meet with us. It could have been for our regular monthly meeting, I can't recall, but when she came that day we had our support worker present so she could back us up in our belief that Nate needed more serious help.

Our support worker had also told us another story. When she had recently taken Nate to the mall, he pulled from his pocket a huge clump of hair. She confronted him about it he explained that he'd pulled it from the vacuum cleaner. She just told him that was disgusting and told him to throw it away. But he refused and put it back in his pocket.

We explained everything that had happened on Saturday. In particular, the story about what Nate had done at the mall really seemed to get the attention of the agency worker.

The worker then asked if she could talk to our older girl, Ericka. Annie went to get her.

"How do you feel about Nate?" the worker asked Ericka.

"He kind of gives me the creeps," Erick answered. "Sometimes he stands really close to me. And I don't like the way he looks at Angel."

31

This concerned us all. Our agency worker told us that she would come back at a later date to interview all the kids in our home.

She returned a week later, on Thursday, June 21. She spoke to Angel, who disclosed that Nate had asked her to have sex with her on more than one occasion. As soon as our worker heard this, she informed me and Annie that she had no choice but to remove Nate from our home. Our kids didn't feel safe with him in the house anymore.

When we learned what Angel had said, we were crushed and broke down crying.

The next task was for the worker to confront Nate about what Angel had told her. Of course, Nate denied it. For someone who didn't know him, his denial would have been believable—but now the worker was starting to catch on.

She made some calls and found an emergency placement elsewhere in the city until the agency could figure out what to do next.

We hugged Nate and reassured him that we still loved him, but that he needed help. Annie then went upstairs with him to help him pack a bag.

In the meantime, I spoke to the worker and gave her some more background about Nate's family history. We had learned through the family members and other acquaintances that incest ran in the family, along with schizophrenia.

Our worker told us that our request for more intensive counselling a year ago couldn't be acted upon, since there had been no evidence. But now they wanted to act?

Was it too late, though? What a beginning to summer!

For the first time in a few years, we all felt safe in our home.

The agency worked to find a treatment centre for Nate, but the only placement available was a bed in September. Until then, he would have to remain in an emergency foster home. This worked out all right, and we continued to pick him up for our family's special events and outings. We tried to give him a sense of normalcy.

We also thought this was all temporary. Once he received help and some counselling, we hoped he could return to our home.

A week and a half later, on the morning of July 4, I went to Johnny's bedroom to wake up Johnny. It was 10:00 a.m. and I was surprised he hadn't gotten up yet. He was always up at the crack of dawn.

But this morning I had to shake him and call his name several times before he even stirred. When I pulled back the bedsheets, I saw that he had Ericka's tablet in bed with him. Ericka was out of the house all week at a children's camp.

"What are you doing with this?" I asked.

Johnny explained that he had snuck downstairs during the night and taken it to listen to music, but he hadn't been able to open it. He didn't know the password.

I took the tablet, gave him his meds, and that was that. Or so I thought.

Later in the morning, when my wife got up, I told her about what had happened. She nterrogated him, at which point he came clean: he'd gotten up in the middle of the night to sneak junk food.

"Why?" Annie asked.

"I was hungry."

This wasn't true, since we always kept fruit and healthy snacks available for the kids if they were hungry. It wasn't about being hungry; it was about being greedy for junk food.

And what about the tablet?

"I used it to take some pictures of myself," Johnny explained. "But I deleted them."

So that was that—again. At least for a while.

Later in the day, my wife received some emails from a friend asking why she had been video-chatting with her daughter at 4:00 in the morning. Our daughter's tablet was registered under Annie's name and email, so her name was the one that showed up when it was used.

We went back to Johnny with more questions and eventually got it out of him that he had accessed the tablet by using a so-called "back door" to open various apps without the password. He had tried chatting with two of Ericka's friends, thankfully without success.

That afternoon Annie checked through the tablet's pictures and opened a whole new can of worms. At 2:30 a.m., he had recorded himself looking intently at the camera. It was too dark, so he turned on the lights. To our shock and disbelief, he was playing with himself, masturbating with the lights on and the door open. He recorded himself for a minute, then turned off the light and the camera.

Would there be any end to this?

When Annie again asked Johnny about what he'd done with the tablet, he repeated what he'd told us about taking some pictures and then deleting them.

We always gave the kids time to come clean about the things they'd done, even though we already knew the truth. We wanted to give them the chance to be honest.

In this case, he didn't take it.

So Annie showed him the video. He was surprised, having thought he'd deleted the video.

We were so upset, just totally floored and heartbroken. We didn't condone masturbation, but we told him if that he was going to do that, he should at least have the decency to either do it in private, like in the shower, or close the door! What if one of the girls had come out of their room at night?

He later revealed that he probably would have done something to them, whether it was his seven-year-old sister or our two-year-old daughter.

We sent him to his room and didn't call the agency again that day. We were too dumbfounded.

The next day, Annie called our worker to inform her of the latest happenings. The worker didn't sound too surprised. Maybe she had expected something like this after removing Nate from our home.

That afternoon, my wife sat down with Johnny to ask some more questions. What he revealed shocked us even more. He told us that he and Nate had been doing things together. When we asked about what kind of things he meant, he told us that Nate had taught him how to masturbate. We had our suspicions that they were doing it with each other, as well as alone in their own beds. He also told us that they had kissed and touched each other inappropriately—and this had been going on for some time.

Before our latest move, the boys had each occupied their own rooms in the basement, which was next to our master bedroom. We eventually caught on that they'd been sneaking into each other's rooms on the weekend because the sound woke us up. But at the time we had just thought they were waking each other up to play with their toys.

How wrong we were.

Johnny went on to admit that Nate, after losing his computer privileges at school, had shown him where to go to access porn sites.

At this point we didn't know whether Johnny was a victim or a sexual predator. Either way, we wanted to get Johnny some immediate counselling to learn the truth.

We didn't call the agency to report this newfound information, because they probably wouldn't have done anything about it anyway. We decided to take matters into our own hands.

Lately, Annie had been speaking with her niece in Toronto. This niece had told her about a visiting pastor from Jamaica who was offering counselling sessions and holding house fellowships, house fellowships being opportunities for believers in Christ to gather with, encourage, and pray for one another. This pastor was a trained counsellor and specialized in sexual behaviours and addictions. He had counselled many people from children to adults. Apparently this pastor was willing to meet with us.

We decided to take a trip to Toronto. We made the long drive the next Saturday and went to meet this pastor. We arrived late that night.

Annie and I listened as Johnny spoke. The pastor started by asking a little bit of the background, and we briefly shared what had transpired in the last few weeks.

Johnny then answered some of the pastor's questions—and what came out once again threw us for a loop.

Johnny revealed that he'd had sex with his sister. As we sat there, all I could think about was that I hoped he was only referring to kissing.

The pastor eventually gave Johnny some good advice to help him overcome these sexual issues, but he would have to be willing to follow the pastor's instructions. Only time would tell if it would work.

We went home at midnight, feeling both physically and emotionally spent. Instead of driving home, we went straight back to Annie's niece's house, where we picked up the other kids. We then crashed at a hotel.

The next morning, we planned to attend a house fellowship where this Jamaican pastor was sharing.

After breakfast, as the kids were getting into the van, I stopped Johnny and asked what he had meant the night before about having sex with his sister.

"Did you mean you kissed her?" I asked.

"Yeah," he said. "That, and anal sex too."

"Is that all?"

"No. I put my private in her private."

"Okay," I calmly told him. "Please get in the van."

Meanwhile, I was screaming in my mind.

Before Annie got in, I told her what Johnny had admitted. We both agreed that we would contact our family doctor as soon as we got home to check out the girls, including our two-year-old.

When we arrived at the house fellowship, I took Ericka, Jewels, Josie, and Johnny and waited outside the house. Annie stayed in the van and talked to Angel.

After the house fellowship Annie and I talked before we headed off to lunch with Annie's family. I honestly had to sit down on the bumper of my van, my legs becoming weak, when Annie revealed what Angel had told her.

Both Nate and Johnny had been doing bad things to her. Nate had told her to do sexy dances and other things. When she refused, he would grab her, pull her into his room, and throw her on the bed. He would touch her inappropriately and perform unmentionable sexual acts.

When I left the siblings in the van, even just for a few minutes to go into a store to pick up a couple of things, he would sexually violate her.

Angel didn't say much about what Johnny had done, perhaps because he was still in the family picture. Later she would come clean about Johnny's actions as well.

We went back to my wife's niece's house for lunch and discussed these horrifying details. We sat in their basement while my wife nursed our newborn, Josie. We broke down and cried. How could this have happened? We had we were vigilant, even overprotective at times.

Our minds raced as we considered whether the boys had done anything to Jewels, our two-year-old. If they could do it to their own flesh and blood, what about our daughter? We weren't too concerned about Ericka, though, since she was twelve and big enough to defend herself. Sexual predators tend to go after those who can't defend or speak up for themselves.

We were so tormented! What should we do now? Should we just close our home and give up on fostering? For years, that's what our family and friends had been telling us to do. Why did we even bother keeping these kids who weren't our own flesh and blood? It was love. Love drove us to do what we did. Love kept us from giving up. When we felt doubt, love kept us together. Love kept us holding on.

But now, we were left to ask ourselves, was love enough?

My wife called a foster parent support group leader to ask for advice. We had known her for a long time and trusted her. She gave Annie some sound advice and we decided to wait until the next morning, a Monday, to contact the agency. We still needed to let this sink in. But how much more of this could we take?

That evening, we went to see another counsellor—this time, a female counsellor who knew the visiting Jamaican pastor. We sat with Angel and this counsellor for a short time and listened as Angel opened up, sharing what had been going on with her two brothers. It was blatantly obvious that a lot of damage had been done over a long period of time.

The next day, we contacted the agency by text message. I left all the correspondence to my wife, as I had little use for them. We were told that Johnny would be apprehended as soon as we returned home from Toronto. Likely, charges would be laid.

At times, Angel had made up far-fetched stories and we had always confronted her about them. But these stories weren't made up. The details were too real and horrific. No way could a seven-year-old little girl come up with these sick fantasies on her own. She had experienced these things in real life.

Johnny came clean by acknowledging that he had told Angel that he would kill her if she didn't have sex with him. But the last time they'd done it, he had also told her that if he ever tried again, she should yell, scream, and run to us for help. Maybe he had realized that what he was doing was wrong.

But the damage was done.

We left very early on Tuesday morning. During the drive, we occasionally broke down in tears, tormented by thoughts of how this could have happened in our own home. We were ministers of the gospel, Christians who lived for God with all our hearts and had done our best to raise our children in the way they should go.

Then we reminded each other of those times when we'd sensed something wrong in our spirits, asking: "Where's Angel? Where's Nate? What are the kids doing?" We pieced together what had happened and when it had started. We believed it had been going on with the boys for five years or more.

But we didn't think Angel had been involved until the previous April, a little over a year ago, during that unscheduled visit with their older siblings. More had gone on that night than we knew. The boys had realized they could get away with it, though, and started preying on their little sister from then on.

If only the agency had done their jobs and performed a full investigation. Perhaps that would have changed the way everything played out.

We got home around 3:00 that afternoon and immediately texted the agency worker, who in turn showed up two hours later. She had lined up an emergency foster home. Physicals would have to be done and statements taken at the police station. Once all the facts were known, there would be charges against the boys, who would then be shipped off to treatment centres.

We called Johnny to come and sit with us. Once the worker started talking about the new information, he only had one question: "When do I leave?" He knew he was going to be taken away.

Annie helped him pack a bag and then took him to his short-term foster home. What a whirlwind! How was this going to end? It didn't look good.

By now we were so drained that we often felt dizzy. The world was spinning around us. We were at wits' end, and the nightmare was only just beginning.

On Wednesday, Angel had her medical appointment. The doctor concluded that everything was still intact and there wasn't any scarring on the buttocks or genitals. That didn't disprove her story. Her brothers weren't fully developed yet, meaning there might not have been full penetration.

Annie took Angel to the police so she could make a statement. We feared she would clam up and "forget" what had happened, but no; she revealed everything that Nate and Johnny had been doing to her. She described what had happened in great detail, shocking the agency's workers. It was even more than the boys had revealed in their own testimonies.

Annie sat with Angel in the questioning room, while the agency workers sat in another room and watched via video.

Afterward, the workers asked Annie how she could sit so calmly without showing any reaction. The workers had been squirming in their seats at some of the details.

"Right now, even after everything the boys did, these kids don't need to feel rejected by their mom," she said. "They need our loving support."

Was this difficult? Of course it was. Annie was torn up inside, but she stayed strong for them on the outside.

Angel revealed that Nate would grab her when she went up to her bedroom to play, throw her down on the bed, and force himself on her, at times touching her private area. If she went downstairs to get a movie from the basement and found Nate playing video games, he would grab her and do sexual things to her. She spoke of how he kissed her, even in the back of our vehicle; we had an eight-seater SUV and the three siblings sat in the back together, Angel between her brothers. We would place her in the middle to separate the boys, because they always poked and bothered each other, but now we realized we had been surrounding her with sexual predators.

The pain in our chests was great. The heartache was overwhelming.

The next day, Thursday, July 12, Annie picked up Johnny from his temporary foster home and brought him to the police station where they took his statement of the events that had taken place over the last few years. He came clean about everything.

After that interview, Annie drove to get Nate. He was visibly shaken, but we had seen him use fake tears in the past to fool people. But it appeared he was genuinely afraid this time. He admitted to almost everything. The truth was finally out.

Following Johnny's interview, while he was waiting in a holding cell, something disturbing happened. He stood in front of the camera and started dancing and singing like crazy. Then he got down on the floor and did push-ups. It was like he was mocking the people watching. Or perhaps he was just putting on a performance. Maybe this all seemed like a joke to him.

However, I think this was his way of coping with the situation.

When both the boys had been interviewed, they were each charged with six charges of sexual interference. There were other charges as well. They would be sent to a different city and placed in separate foster homes to await their placement in a specialized facility to treat their addictions and other issues.

Here's the kicker: the agency had told us the previous day that they would transport both boys in the same vehicle, as there was a shortage of workers. One would sit in the front while the other sat in the back.

Pardon my language, but was the agency demented? Didn't they realize what had taken place here? After all these boys had done to each other and their little sister, why were they being allowed to ride together? Was there no common sense in the decision-making process?

After discussing the situation with me, Annie volunteered to drive one of the boys to their next home. Seeing as Johnny was the last to leave, she offered to take him, as long as the agency agreed. They did and offered to pay for Annie's mileage, gas, and hotel.

On Friday, July 13, my wife left at 6:00 a.m. for a ten-hour ride. She picked up Johnny at his foster home and hit the road.

For the first half of the trip, all he talked about was how much he missed the two new friends he had made. He had only been at the temporary foster home for two days and considered these boys his friends. Here we were, having poured nine years of love, nurturing, and compassion into this boy—and all he missed was a couple of teenagers he had only known for forty-eight hours!

As they neared their destination, Johnny told his mom that he felt a little anxious about the move. He also shared more details about the last few years and the sexual abuse. It was disturbing to hear him describe himself as the "lookout man" while Nate was abusing his sister. Whether it was in the backseat of the van, downstairs when she came to get a movie, or upstairs when she was in her room, Johnny would watch in case anyone came along. He would warn Nate if he was about to get caught.

Annie was so distressed after she dropped off Johnny that she called me on her cell phone. She was crying and barely made any sense. I told her to stop at a hotel and rest; she could drive back in the morning.

But she didn't want to be away from home.

When she was four hours from home, she texted me to ask whether she should keep driving or stop. I told her to stop. She could drive the rest of the way the next day and meet us at a family church camp we would be attending for the next two weeks.

Annie signed off for the night and I assumed she had booked a hotel room. But at 1:30 in the morning, she texted me and told me how much she loved and missed me.

"Me too," I wrote back.

"Don't be afraid. I'm there with you."

That's when I heard something. Thinking it was one of the girls getting up to use the washroom, I got up to check. As I did, Annie texted again.

"Open the door. I'm outside."

As if!?

I opened my bedroom door and there she was, standing in front of me. Crazy girl! She could have given me a heart attack! At least we knew that my heart was good.

The two weeks we spent at family camp were difficult, with everything still fresh in our hearts, minds, and spirits. We did, however, speak to some people we trusted and they prayed for us. In talking with my district pastor, he shared with me that he was a child of incest; his broken family had gone through much pain and healing through the years.

I was very concerned for Annie. She was constantly fatigued and worried she was losing her nutrients from nursing Josie. Then she came down with a cold that proved hard to shake. She decided to book an appointment with her doctor to get checked out and have some bloodwork done.

That's when I knew there must be something wrong, because she really didn't like doctors. Who does?

While at the camp, Jewels had diarrhea for several days and began to develop a rash on her bottom. When my wife was putting cream on her behind one day, she asked Jewels if anyone had ever touched her there before. To Annie's horror, she mentioned Nate, Johnny, and Angel. That concerned us.

The next day, while taking Jewels to the washroom at the mess hall, I asked her if anyone had touched her. Again, she said that Nate, Johnny, and Angel had.

For a third day in a row, we asked her something similar—and again she mentioned those three names.

I called our family doctor and told him we would be coming to town to get Jewels checked out. We were starting to suspect that the boys had done something to her.

Not only that, but we put up our guard with Angel too. How damaged had she become at the abusive hands of her brothers? Was she now acting out as well?

We went to town that day and saw the doctor. He examined her and assured us that everything was fine. Jewels was in perfect health, very strong and healthy for her age.

Still, we were now suspicious of Angel.

Some days during those two weeks at camp, we were very emotional and upset with the older kids. At times Jimmy, Ericka, and Angel seemed lazy, taking shortcuts with their chores and lying about simple things. Under other circumstances, it might not have bothered us so much, but we were so emotionally drained and feeling sick. At one point, Annie even thought she was on the verge of an emotional breakdown.

But as hard as things were, we knew God would see us through and strengthen us. He would bring healing.

The preaching at camp lifted us. One speaker had been talking about the prodigal son, revealing a lot more richness to the story than I had ever heard before. We trusted that the word of God would see us through.

We remember an interaction we'd had with the police officer who had led the case against Nate and Johnny.

"There's nothing more you could have done," the officer had told Annie. "You are evident y a good home. You've done everything you could for these boys. How do you keep it all together?"

My wife had taken the opportunity to share her faith. "It's my faith in God… and prayer."

I had a similar experience with our foster care worker. She asked if I had always gone to church, and this led to a chance to talk about my faith too.

God has a plan. Even when we have no idea what's going on, God is still in control, no matter what.

AS WE LOOKED back over the past nine years, we slowly put the pieces together of this shattered puzzle. Without a complete picture of the puzzle, we couldn't make sense of what had happened.

There's an old saying that says, "You can't see the forest for the trees." This refers to being able to see the details, but not the big picture.

In our case, we saw the trees, but not the forest. Now the bigger picture was coming into focus. We could recall numerous instances of peculiar behaviour from the kids over the years.

When Nate was four years old and in junior Kindergarten, from time to time he would pull down his pants in class and show off his privates. One might think, "Hey, that's not normal." And if the agency had done its job back then, things might not have turned out so bad. They dismissed this as playful, attention-seeking behaviour. Well, it obviously didn't get the attention of the agency workers! Thinking back now, they should have talked to Nate about this and asked why he would do such a thing. But that would have meant being proactive, which we felt the agency didn't do.

At age five, Annie recalled catching Nate and Jimmy, who was one year older, showing each other their privates. When Annie contacted the agency about it, she was told, "Oh, they're just boys.

They're just curious." No action was taken. We just separated the boys and managed to give them their own rooms.

At age six, we caught Nate in Ericka's room when she was only four. They were playing the "kissing game," pretending to be Mommy and Daddy. Again, the agency thought nothing of it. According to them, this was just a part of growing up, playing and exploring.

Since this incident happened afterhours, we called the on-call afterhours agency worker. When my wife explained that she'd caught them kissing, the worker laughed at Annie and said, "Are you serious? What do you want me to do?" She didn't take us seriously and made a joke out of our call.

We reported everything that happened because we thought that was the protocol and our responsibility. We were doing our due diligence, exercising a reasonable amount of care to prevent harm. We didn't want these incidents to escalate to something more serious in the future.

Did they listen? No, they quite often laughed at us.

Their action so enraged me that I told Annie we should file a complaint.

"Why?" Annie said, laughing. "They'll just deny it anyway."

Nate, Johnny, and Ericka were playing outside one winter's day when Nate was seven. As I watched through the window, to my disbelief, I watched him pretend to shove a stick up Ericka's bum when she bent over. She didn't know, since he didn't touch her with the stick, but it was a little disturbing. I didn't even bother reporting it.

At age eight, we caught Nate humping a dog from behind. Again, the agency didn't bat an eyelash at this.

When Nate was ten, he received his school laptop with assistive technology. I set it up with particular websites that would help him with math, language, spelling, writing, etc. But that Christmas, Jimmy's older brother came over for an overnight visit. This older brother was fourteen and showed Nate how to access porn on the laptop while Jimmy slept.

This was like opening pandora's box. It was a downward spiral from there. Pornography took hold of Nate's life for the next five years until he was finally taken away and charged with sex crimes.

For someone with fetal alcohol syndrome, it's difficult to make educated decisions. They have no restraints. If they try a drink of alcohol, they become alcoholics. If they try gambling, they get addicted to gambling. If they try drugs, they're hooked. If they view porn... well, you get the picture.

When Nate was eleven, we headed to Toronto to stay with friends during the March break. One day we happened to use Nate's computer and saw that someone had accessed porn on it. Nate vehemently denied this and blamed his friend, who we were staying with.

"He must have gone on the laptop when I wasn't around, or when I was sleeping," Nate insisted.

We took his word for it.

But later, we thought about the incident more and found that it didn't sit well with us. Annie checked with our friends, and they said their son hadn't gone on the computer. So we knew it must have been Nate. As a result, he missed out on attending a motocross event at Rogers Centre.

Later that same year, when Nate was eleven and Johnny was ten, we delivered our very first child, Jewels. When Annie and I were at the hospital, the kids stayed at our friend's house. My friend was a big kid himself, but we felt pretty safe about leaving the kids with him and his family.

But we later learned this trip marked the first time Johnny did anything to his sister. He kissed her and touched her inappropriately.

Then came the incident of discovering the hiding place in Nate's boxspring, which I already mentioned. We freaked out.

Despite all the warning signs, we were still in the dark about the sexual activity taking place between the brothers.

After our big move, which we took to provide the children with more opportunities, I started teaching at a private school. We enrolled all of our school-aged children. As previously discussed, Nate used this as an opportunity to access porn again. He was caught more than once and didn't learn his lesson. An addict rarely does.

I was floored when Nate didn't seem to show any remorse. He just kept going like everything was perfect. He didn't react to the consequences of his actions. He would just give us the silent treatment and treat us like we were the ones in the wrong.

I was so frustrated by the agency's seeming lack of interest in treating Nate's porn addiction. Despite what they said, it wasn't just a normal part of growing up.

There was a story in the news around this time of a lawyer who had been sent to jail for accessing and distributing child porn. In his case, it had started off innccently, with looking at pictures of men and women. The photos got more erotic before continuing on to child porn. The addiction snowballed from there.

A friend of mine lived nearby to that lawyer and could remember seeing the man put out his garbage every morning. Children would walk by his front door and go to school just down the street, not knowing that they were so close to a pedophile.

A person doesn't become a pedophile overnight. It's progressive, a slippery slope. Once you start, it's hard to stop.

Over the years, the issues escalated. We constantly reminded Nate that if he kept viewing porn, it would control him. We reminded him of his potential to achieve great things in life. He had so many excellent skills. He was determined and athletic. He was an awesome goaltender who could easily have made it to the big leagues one day. He even excelled at lacrosse and football.

Despite all this potential, he threw it away in favour of an addiction to porn. We often framed it as a choice: "Nate, it's either family or pornography. What will you choose? If you continue down this road of addiction, you will lose everything." He always told us that he would choose wisely, but that's not the choice he ended up making.

# 7

## House of Love or House of Horror?

AFTER EVERYTHING THAT had come out, all these revelations of total and utter disgust and disbelief, my wife asked me, "Eddie, has this been a house of love or a house of horrors?" She was questioning whether we had really been the loving household we had assumed we were. Had we been there to provide protection, support, love, and compassion for these children in our care? Did we really know how to be good parents, able to raise them in the ways they should go?

I felt we had done everything in our power to ensure we did our best to raise our children to become strong, healthy, loving human beings. We had been raising seven children the same way, showing no favouritism to any of them.

Many years ago, I heard someone say, "More is caught than is taught." In other words, you can tell a person something loving, but it's more memorable to see love in action. That's what compassion is: love in action. Our children saw how well Annie and I treated each other. They saw how we treated others. They saw us do the best we could to live for God through His son Jesus Christ. They saw when we got upset or impatient, but they also saw us ask for forgiveness when we were in the wrong. We would apologize and try and become more patient as time went on.

"We're Christians," we would say. "But we're not perfect."

When an agency worker came by for a visit, Angel came up and excitedly showed her the new Bible we had just bought for her. This worker was amazed that a child could get so excited about a Bible. The kids really loved God.

Annie and I hadn't always been raised in church. We weren't proud of every aspect of our lives, but we were thankful that God had saved us and given us the opportunity to raise other people's children.

Many people don't believe in foster care and being foster parents, but it's very biblical.

> Pure and genuine religion in the sight of God the
> Father means caring for orphans and widows in
> their distress and refusing to let the world corrupt
> you. (James 1:27)

This scripture speaks of caring for orphans, those who don't have parents. Now that sounds like fostering to me!

We gave everything in our power to care for these children. Our children have visited every province from Newfoundland to British Columbia. They've been to major league baseball games, hockey games, and motocross events. Every child dreams of the circus and, well, we've been to a few of those too. Don't even mention all the midways and fairs! We've stayed in fancy hotels, gone to campgrounds, and swam in the Atlantic and Pacific Oceans. Been there, done that. We haven't withheld anything from our children.

People have told us, "Wait until you have your own children. You're going to love them even more. It's a different love!"

I can honestly say, after having two of our own children, that it is *not* a different love. The love we have for our biological children and the love we have for our adopted children is the same. We love our children, period. It's an unconditional love. We still love Nate and Johnny, even after all they've done. My wife has always told them, "No matter where life takes you, no matter the choices you make and where you end up, we want to be your children's grandparents."

God has revealed his unconditional love to us, so maybe that's why we have so much love to offer.

Our family has been all about dancing, laughing, practical jokes, tears, joy, heart-to-hearts, and sharing our dreams and pains with each other. I recently heard a minister say, "If we didn't care, it wouldn't hurt." Love does hurt, and it's because we care.

Psalm 30:5 says, *"Weeping may last through the night, but joy comes with the morning."*

There's an old expression that says that the sun always shines after the rain. In other words, this too shall pass. But things were so fresh and painful in that season of our lives that it was hard to see the day ahead.

Despite this, when we reminded ourselves of all we had done, we couldn't help but ask ourselves, "Is our house a house of horrors?" When the sexual experimentation initially started between Nate and Johnny, what had Johnny thought? We knew that Nate was the instigator. He had started this chain of events...

Or had he? We'll address this further a little later.

Had Johnny been scared about getting into trouble if he said anything about what Nate was showing him? Did he think it was natural? Did he think it was terrible? Did he enjoy it from the start?

We don't know. Only Johnny might be able to answer those questions one day.

Then there was Angel. We still couldn't figure out why she hadn't ever come forward to speak up about what was going on. She was close with us, and even closer with her adopted sister Ericka. She hadn't said anything to Erick either. In fact, she had said that her brothers never threatened her. And yet Johnny had admitted that he'd threatened her life if she didn't have sex with him. That sounded like a threat to me!

Had she thought it was okay because Johnny was her brother? Had she been scared? Why hadn't she screamed or fought back? Had she come to enjoy the attention and acts her brothers were doing?

Perhaps only counselling and time would tell. She was only seven, so our hope and prayer was that she would get the help she needed to get over this traumatic time of her life.

The agency told us that she would need grief and loss counselling over her two brothers being taken away. Of course they would say that. To us, she seemed more at ease now that they were gone.

One day, Annie asked her, "Angel, if there's one thing in the whole wide world you could have, what would it be?"

"To have no more workers," she replied.

Wow! You would think a seven-year-old girl would want a puppy, or go to Disney Land, or get a new bike. Instead Angel just wanted to be out of the system, out of the agency's care.

# 8

## Falling through the Cracks

IN THE FOSTER system, people were constantly coming and going, both children and agency workers. It was a revolving door and corrupt system, cold and heartless. The system was supposed to make its decisions in the best interests of children, but the track record we observed said otherwise.

I recently spoke to a friend who worked in pediatric medicine. Over the years, she became so hardened against the agency. Abuse had obviously taken place based on the reviews and detailed medical reports she'd seen. Time after time, she saw X-rays of children showing broken bones, fractured limbs, and bruises, all inflicted by adults. She told us that these reports were often thrown to the wayside, evidence disregarded on the grounds of very shaky stories. She saw children go back to the very same homes where abuse had happened, only to come back with new wounds.

Over time, we learned more about the family Nate, Johnny, and Angel came from. When their older brother Josiah had been a baby, he'd been molested by his uncle. Nothing was done when he was taken to the hospital. No reports were filed. The uncle wasn't turned in. To this day, their uncle is still in the picture. Based on the stories we've heard, it seems like he is probably still molesting children. The older sister, Gerry, has since had her own child and has said she never leaves her baby with that uncle!

It makes me wonder. When Nate and Johnny came into care at the ages of three and two, had they been molested by their uncle? The evidence seems to point in that direction. What if the agency had acted twenty years ago, in the incident of Josiah's abuse as a baby? What if they had stepped in or at least investigated the incident? Would things have turned out differently?

We may never know.

I couldn't help but wonder whether the agency had ever been told the complete story of what had taken place in this family. Were they even aware of why the boys had gone into care? Most likely not, we think. We were never given the complete history of this family. The only reason we know the details we do is because we conducted our own investigation.

Would the boys get the help they needed? Would they reoffend? Our hope and prayer has always been that they would get help. We told them to be honest with their counsellors, themselves, and God. What happened next was up to them.

Years ago, when we fostered a pair of siblings while living in another province, we asked the agency, as well as the mother, whether we could adopt the children. There was a boy and a girl, and we wanted to adopt both.

The mother would only allow us to adopt the boy, not the girl. We couldn't do that, so both siblings eventually went back to the mother. To make a long story short, they both went through a horrendous time. That little girl now has about six children of her own and all of them are in foster care. As a young mother, she wasn't given the supports and resources she needed. Instead the agency just apprehends her children.

Come to think of it, that's why many families don't ask for help from governmental agencies. They're fearful that their children will be taken away.

We told Nate and Johnny that if they didn't make better choices, the agency might one day take them away. We warned them of children who were sent to other foster homes, many of them specialized for troubled youth. We had heard they would drug them up and just keep giving them more medication. These children basically became zombies, living in a catatonic state for much of their lives until they aged out of the system.

Johnny was sent to a specialized foster home like this. When Annie dropped him off, she asked questions concerning his meds. Annie told them that he only took Concerta in the morning, a slow-release form of Ritalin.

"Doesn't he take anything at night?" they asked.

That kind of confirmed to us that they used medication to control a lot of the children's behaviour.

# Victimizing the Victim

ANNIE AND I enjoy watching police and legal procedurals on TV. One of our favourite shows is *Law and Order SVU: Special Victims Unit*. The show details the stories of those who have been raped or molested. At times, the show's fictional defence attorneys will try and question the innocence of a rape victim, perhaps by attacking their choice of clothing, makeup, and behaviour before the incident took place.

"Well, why were you in that place at that time?" they might ask. "Wouldn't you say you were dressed rather provocatively? Witnesses have said you made advances on the defendant in the past. Isn't it true that you just wanted to get back at my client?"

In other words, attorneys would try to paint these victims as being partially to blame for what happened to them.

Although this was a TV show, the same thing happens all too often in real life—more than we'd like to admit. The victim is victimized all over again.

By August, not even two months from the full unravelling, we were still in a haze of confusion and disbelief over the events that had taken place in our home. But at least we felt as though the children in our home were safe. The boys were in specialized homes getting better care than we had been able to give them. We kept holding on to God, relying on Him to get us through one day at a time.

We were in need of a break, so we decided to go shopping for a camper. Our kids loved camping. The last time we'd gone camping had been in 2010 when we took six weeks to drive all the way to Newfoundland to see my family. We took two weeks to get there and then slowly made our way through the Maritimes.

When I say that we went camping, I mean *camping*. We went old school, with a tent, blow-up mattresses, and a portable camp stove. You know, real camping!

But now we were ready to make the big jump to a travel trailer. We wanted to go camping in style.

We showered that morning, excited to look for a camper. Our plan was to drive to another community, an hour away, where we thought we might get a better deal.

Just before we were about to leave, the phone rang. It was the agency. They told us that they needed to see us for a meeting.

Now what?

That was our first thought. I tried to calm Annie: "Maybe they just want to check on us to see how we're doing."

So off we went in search of a trailer, but we decided to shop locally instead of travelling an hour away. We looked at a few options, then filled out some forms to see if we would be approved for financing.

While we were filling out the forms, Annie was very agitated. She looked very hot and flustered, as though she just wanted out.

"I'm going outside," she told me.

I honestly don't know what happened with that application. I don't even remember exactly how the rest of the morning went. It's all a bit of a blur.

We went to the meeting with the agency and took all the kids with us. When we got there, we were once again sucker-punched. The agency told us that they wanted to take Angel out of our care as well and send her to another foster home in another region.

When would this ever end?

We were shocked and outraged. How could they possibly do this to her? It was like they were punishing her for what her brothers had done. Just like on that TV show, they were victimizing the victim. She had been molested by her own brothers and now these workers wanted to remove her from the only loving family she had ever known.

I'm pretty sure we broke down right there and then. We were irate.

The agency wanted to remove her from our home by blaming us for what had happened. If we'd had more safety measures in place, this wouldn't have happened, so they said. I'm pretty sure we pointed out that they had turned us down every time we'd asked for help. We had warned them about the boys' tendencies, especially Nate. The workers had just laughed at us or blown off our reports, saying that these behaviours were just a part of growing up.

We also reminded them that if it hadn't been for them allowing the three kids to have an unsupervised sleepover, which had never been part of the plan, Angel wouldn't have been sexually molested in the first place.

65

But it was all about them covering up their own mistakes. They figured that by taking Angel out of our family's care, they could make this all go away.

They underestimated the love we had for our children. No, they weren't our biological children, but we had raised them as our own and to this very day we still love them as our own.

We refused to give up without a fight! We didn't want Angel to think any of what had happened was her fault. That's the very message the agency would have been sending by taking her out of our home—that she was at fault, not the victim. We wouldn't stand for it.

Looking back, it's a blur. But I do remember going to the local Indigenous friendship centre to see some of the counsellors and support workers. When we walked in, I met a good friend of mine who worked there. He was a brother in the Lord and knew the struggles we had been facing. I remember telling him that the agency wanted to take Angel away.

Then I broke down. I literally began to wail. It was a gut-wrenching cry I had never experienced before in my life. I'm gentle and I don't mind shedding a few tears, but this was painful. From the depths of my soul, I was broken. Everything we had gone through came pouring out. I believe we went to the friendship centre to check on what kind of support they could muster for us in order to keep Angel.

During the meeting, we had Angel come in. That's when we told her what the agency wanted to do. She cried in Annie's arms and said, "No! I don't want to go!" She was finally safe from the ones who had harmed her. She was free from her abusers.

We wanted the best for Angel, and we felt that was to stay in our care so we could provide the stable, loving home she so desperately needed. We were her mom and dad. Why would the agency want to take her away from the only people who had ever loved her? We were the only parents she'd ever had. She hadn't developed any relationship with her biological parents. So why victimize her again by ripping her away from us?

It was all about the agency covering their own tracks.

They finally agreed to leave her in our care. At least now she was safe, and we could move on together and take the road to healing.

# 10

## Stretching and Proving

A PART OF the healing took us on the literal road to the Ottawa valley—in particular, a little place called Cobden at the Noah's Ark Campground. Having been turned down for the financing of a trailer, we did the next best thing: bought a nice big tent, dug out all our camping gear, and hit the road.

We spent a week at the campground and spent some much-needed quality time together. Josie was only three months and boy did she like to sleep! She would fall asleep at 8:00 at night and sleep right through until 8:00 the next morning. She wouldn't even wake up for her bottle!

That August, we also spent some time with Annie's family in Toronto. While there, we spoiled the kids by taking them to a Blue Jays game, the Medieval Times dinner theatre, Santa's Village, and Canada's Wonderland amusement park. We had gone through a literal hell and needed the much-deserved vacation.

We felt like a rubber band that had been stretched almost to the breaking point, and now it wouldn't snap back into place. But the God we serve is more than able, by His grace, to sustain us. Consider what 1 Corinthians 10:13 says:

> The temptations in your life are no different from what others experience. And God is faithful. He will not allow the temptation to be more than you can stand. When you are tempted, he will show you a way out so that you can endure.

God knows how much we can handle. He knows how far we can be stretched before we break. The apostle Paul went on to say, in 2 Corinthians 12:9,

> Each time he said, "My grace is all you need. My power works best in weakness." So now I am glad to boast about my weaknesses, so that the power of Christ can work through me.

Paul was basically saying that God is glorified through our weaknesses, trials, and hardships. His strength and love shine through our lives during our weakest times. He sustains us.

We took pretty much all of August to relax and refresh ourselves, not just from everything we had been through in the past two months, but from the previous nine years of caring for Nate and Johnny. We had poured so much of ourselves into them. It was like pieces of our hearts had been removed. Now we were trying our best to get our lives back on track with some sense of normalcy.

We got back home at the end of August. The private school where I had taught had booked me and my fellow teachers to receive first aid and CPR training. The two-day course was paid for by the school board, and it was very much appreciated.

School was scheduled for the following week.

However, the day after the CPR training, I received a call from the chairman of the board with some devastating news: they were closing the school permanently due to declining enrolment. At least we would get a month and a half of severance pay.

As they say, "When it rains, it pours." Once again we felt stretched out like a rubber band. After everything we'd gone through, now I was out of a job, with no way to pay the bills, especially with Annie still on maternity leave. Our finances were in dire straits.

We couldn't believe it! Where had we gone wrong?

I went to the unemployment centre, looking for a job. I couldn't find another teaching position, nor anything as a janitor or educational assistant. Instead I found funding to earn my heavy equipment license so I could drive transport. I got hired right out of trucking school for a short-haul route that allowed me to be home every night, but it wouldn't start until January. That was six months away. By that time, we would have maxed out our credit cards and line of credit, using anything and everything to stay afloat. But like David said of the Lord, *"I have never seen the godly abandoned or their children begging for bread"* (Psalm 37:25). God always seemed to provide.

The next six months were unsettling. Although Nate and Johnny had been removed from our home, they did return to our city a few times for court appearances. Annie went to see them. We still loved them and they still needed our support.

But something was up with Angel, who was displaying odd behaviour. Perhaps she was acting out due to the damage done by her siblings. Maybe she had emotional scars. We didn't know what to think.

From time to time, Jewels told us that Angel was touching her. We dismissed this at first, thinking that Jewels was overreacting or making up stories. We should have taken her more seriously.

By January, Annie and I came to the decision that Angel needed another home. And we needed to close our home to fostering. It was one of the most difficult decisions we ever made. We loved Angel and wanted to keep her, but she needed help we couldn't provide. She needed a home with two loving parents who could give her the one-on-one attention she needed.

We were exhausted and broken. On top of that Annie, was so stressed out and aggravated over everything that she was getting sick. She had constant headaches and pain, and now tests had shown she had fatty tumours on her liver that were increasing in size and possibly cancerous. All the turmoil had taken its toll.

We love our children, but we know they will one day grow up, move out, and leave us. For any married couple, after raising a family it will just be the two of them standing together. It's important not to allow children to create a divide in the relationship. Sometimes you have to make a decision based on the welfare of your spouse.

We called the agency and told them about our decision. We had been through the wringer and had come to the end. As much as we didn't want to give Angel up, we had to do it. Her strange actions were becoming more erratic and we didn't know what she was capable of. So for the safety of our baby and toddler, and for our own health and well-being, we had to close our home. But we wanted to help the agency find a good home for her. We didn't just want her to be dropped into a group home.

They found a young couple who couldn't have any children of their own, much like we had been at the beginning. They were desperate to provide love to a young child, preferably a girl. This couple lived on a farm in the Huntsville area and were well-off. They were an approved foster home and wanted to adopt, too.

Once all the details were worked out, we spoke to this couple by chat and they showed us around their house. They showed Angel where her room would be, and it even had a beautifully made plaque of her name hanging on the bedroom door. They showed us a pile of presents for her from their parents and others in their family. They hadn't even met Angel and were already showering her with gifts and showing her how much she would be loved!

This was an answered prayer for us.

It was a tearful goodbye, a true melancholy moment. We loved Angel so much, but we knew she would be greatly loved at her new home.

We kept in touch for a few months. Her new adoptive parents allowed her to call, and sometimes Annie spoke with Angel's new mom. Angel had her own pony—yes, her very own pony—a four-wheeler, a room full of toys, and a lot of love.

However, her newfound parents slowly cut us off. They blocked Annie on social media and no longer took our calls. If we did get a call from Angel, she had to be sneaky about it.

"I have to let you go now," she would say in a rush. "Mom is coming!"

I'm not sure why they cut us off. Maybe they wanted us out of her life so they could be the only ones she turned to. Or perhaps the agency told Angel's new parents stories about us that made us look bad. That's our suspicion anyway.

We haven't heard from her in years. We only hope that she doesn't feel like we abandoned her. Maybe one day she'll come looking for us, either in person or online. We can only hope.

Annie sneakily goes onto Angel's social media pages sometimes, just to check on her. She doesn't want to reach out or interfere in her life. But we still pray for her and love her. Maybe one day…

• • •

In September 2013, we received a call from the agency telling us that they wanted to drop by. Annie started to panic. Now what did they want?

I tried to calm her fears.

"Maybe the worker wants to check on us," I told her. "It's been a year since everything happened. Maybe they want to see if there's anything they can do for us."

But if there's one thing through all these years I've come to trust, it's Annie's intuition. She senses things. I believe God has given her that ability.

And in this case, she was right again.

The agency came by to tell us there was an open investigation into some allegations Nate and Johnny had made about us.

Actually, she didn't say who specifically had made the allegations.

When would this end?

The worker now wanted to talk to Jewels, Ericka, and Jimmy alone to ask them questions. We had never done anything wrong to any of the more than forty children who had stayed with us. We had only loved, nurtured, and ra sed them like our own flesh and blood. But now we were under the microscope.

The worker asked Jimmy and Ericka specific questions about how we had treated Nate and Johnny while they were in our care. I remember Ericka crying because she was so upset that the boys would make up stories about us. Jimmy couldn't believe it either and told the worker we were good parents.

The agency also wanted to drop by the kids' schools to check on them from time to time.

"Absolutely not!" we told them. No way did we want the agency going into the school to interrogate our children. There was such stigma about agency workers in the school. We didn't want Jimmy and Ericka's friends to mark them as problem kids.

If the agency wanted to speak with our kids, they would have to do it in our home.

Their investigation went on for about four months. We were on pins and needles, always fearing that the agency would show up on our doorstep and take all our children away. It was a nightmare. We tensed up every time the phone rang.

Even all these years later, that investigation still haunts us.

When the agency finally showed up on our doorstep just before Christmas, our hearts sank. We didn't know what to expect. They had come to tell us that our case was closed. What a relief! Although we wished she had just called.

At times we beat ourselves up. Had all these bad things happened because we were bad parents? Had we broken these kids? Had we been too hard on them? Had we forced Christianity on them and caused them to rebel?

But it wasn't us. We had done our best, never withholding anything they needed—especially love. They made their own bad choices to land themselves in their current situation.

# 11

## Jumping Ship

Annie's mom passed away. It had been a few years of heartache and continuously trusting in God. He proved Himself time after time, always coming through and strengthening us, giving us hope through His son Jesus Christ.

Soon after that, we found out that our friend Eli had been diagnosed with cancer. His prognosis wasn't looking good. He was receiving chemo treatment in Sudbury and had to travel back and forth from our city. Their apartment wasn't good for their health, since it had mould and they had to climb a lot of stairs.

He and his family came to live with us. We stood with them during this battle.

The previous summer, Jimmy had gone to an air cadet camp. He seemed to be acting differently around this time, but we just assumed it was hormones. To make a long story short, it turned out that Jimmy had been doing drugs, lying, and selling his stuff for quite some time. In fact, it had likely been happening for close to a year. He was a smart, handsome boy with a kind and generous heart and a bright future ahead of him. But the lying got so bad that he started to believe his own lies.

With Eli and his wife Roz as our witnesses, we sat down with Jimmy and gave him an ultimatum: "Jimmy, it's either your family or drugs. You can't have both."

He went upstairs, packed a bag, and proceeded to leave.

"Where are you going?" I asked.

"I don't know. I'll figure it out."

"You don't have to go. We're not kicking you out."

But he was so addicted by this point that nothing we said could change his mind.

Jimmy came back a few weeks later, but it didn't last. He packed up again a short time later and left—for good this time. He was only fifteen years old and in Grade Ten! He threw away a great future.

He left our house and bounced around for a while between his friends, crashing wherever he could find a place to sleep.

After a few months of this, we contacted his biological aunt— well, she was more of a cousin of the family—and told her what Jimmy was up to. We asked if she would be willing to take him in and give him a place to stay.

She gladly agreed to help him out.

He went to the reservation and stayed with her and her husband. Annie kept in touch with his aunt, and they talked regularly. But after a while, she stopped contacting Annie. Once again we assumed Jimmy had told her horror stories about how mean we were to him and how we had mistreated him. She seemed to just cut us off without even asking for our side of the story.

Later that fall, the agency again got in contact to inform us that Jimmy had made accusations. Because of these allegations, the local police had to get involved. If I'm not mistaken, the police officer who conducted the ensuing investigation was the same officer who had been involved with us when Nate and Johnny were charged.

Here we were again, once again under the threat of having our children taken away on account of false accusations.

The investigation went on for a short time. Basically, the police ended up concluding there was no cause to believe any of the accusations were true. It was just a matter of an angry child making up stories about his parents.

I clearly remember Ericka, Jimmy's biological sister, getting so upset when the agency and the police questioned us. How could he do this after Nate and Johnny had broken our hearts and almost destroyed our family? She was shocked at the stories Jimmy made up about us. Her brother had really hurt her.

Ericka assured the investigators that no way could we have done anything to hurt Jimmy. We loved them! She had a lot of hate and bitterness towards her brother, but we told her not to feel that way; it was the drugs distorting his mind. We told her to pray for him.

When I saw Jimmy again a few years ago, in 2020, I almost didn't recognize him. He was gaunt, lifeless, and pail, freshly kicked out of his girlfriend's house, whom he'd left to raise their six-month-old baby. He had also been kicked off the reservation for selling drugs. He didn't appear to have much of a future. He was still spreading rumours about how bad and wicked we were.

I recently read a post he wrote on social media about how he was raised in foster care with no one to care for him, love him, or be there for him. Just like countless others, Jimmy played the victim. He wouldn't take responsibility for any of his own choices.

Well, we know the truth. We can sleep at night knowing that we loved him when no one else did. I guess he doesn't remember going on four vacations a year. I guess he doesn't remember the motor-cross rallies, the Raptors games, the Blue Jays games, the video games, the guitars he got to play, the flatscreen TVs, etc. The list could go on and on.

But most importantly, and saddest of all, he doesn't seem to remember the unconditional love we gave him. But we pray one day he will come to his senses.

• • •

By 2015, Nate, Johnny, Angel, and Jimmy were all gone. Only three years before, we had purchased a big house to accommodate our growing family—more than two thousand square feet, five bedrooms, three bathrooms, and a fully finished basement.

Instead our family had shrunk. We were down to three children—Ericka, Jewels, and Josie.

But things didn't stop there. Ericka was the next to jump ship.

Her attitude began changing. She started being sneaky about things, skipping out on the boxing class we had signed her up for. I went to watch her box one evening and discovered she wasn't there. Apparently she had been very sporadic in her attendance.

She was also getting into trouble at school. She would skip class, throw temper tantrums, and run away. One time she left with one of the school's laptops. It was a long litany of misbehaviour. We loved her and tried talking to her, laying out the consequences of what she was doing. We kept encouraging her, too.

The breaking point came on New Year's Eve. We drove to pick her up from her job at a local coffee shop at 10:30 p.m. so we could take her with us to a sliding party and bonfire. When we showed up at her workplace, though, everyone looked very confused. Ericka had called in that day and said she wouldn't be in to work. And yet she had left the house for her shift at her regular time.

It turned out she had gone to her friend's house where she'd planned to party and drink for New Year's instead of being with her family.

She had been sneaking around behind our backs. But in the end, just as the Bible says, a person's sin will find them out. It always does.

So we went to the New Year's party with our church family and tried to have fun, but it was difficult.

I can't remember exactly when we next saw Ericka, but it was a few days later and she was hungover. Needless to say, we had a discussion with her and warned her about this lifestyle. We tried reminding her of what had happened with her brother. His lifestyle had taken him from our family; he'd chosen drugs over the love of his family. She protested vehemently that she was nothing like her brother. It sounded like she still had some resentment towards him.

And yet she was doing exactly what Jimmy had done.

So she came home, slept, got over her hangover, and started feeling better... only to hang out with her "friends" again and start the cycle all over.

After that, she never came home again. She moved in with a friend's family and even had the gall to ask whether we could sign over our parental authority so her friend's mom could receive her child allowance. She basically wanted out of our lives and out of our family.

So we did just that. You can't force someone to love you, and you can't force them to stay if they don't want to.

Since then, as far as we know, Ericka has been living off and on with her biological aunt and uncle. The situation has been tumultuous at best. Currently, she has a "boyfriend," and I use that term loosely. He just got out of jail and they're both couch-surfing.

She has gone down the same path as Jimmy, Nate, and Johnny before her. She made false accusations against us, too. And of course, at the end of the day, we have been proven innocent on all charges. God has vindicated us time and time again.

# 12

## "God Hates Mommies and Daddies!"

BEFORE YOU GET too worked up about this chapter's title, let me explain. I'll start by telling a true story I heard a few years ago at a church service.

A visiting preacher from the United Kingdom shared about a loving family in his congregation who had been very faithful in their walk with the Lord over the years. This inspiring family had been very active in the church, getting involved, being charitable and compassionate, and loving the Lord with all their hearts.

Their daughter, who was in her early twenties, had made the decision to go into full-time ministry and was headed to Kenya. The family hosted a celebration dinner for their daughter and invited the entire family, as well as this pastor.

Before the meal, the family asked the pastor to bless the food and pray a blessing over their daughter. Of course the pastor agreed; it would be his honour and privilege.

However, just as he was about to pray, he felt God prompt him in his spirit to say, "God hates mommies and daddies!" Well, he couldn't believe it. How could he say that?

This pastor had a very close relationship with the Lord and had heard the Lord speak to him on many occasions. At times

God prompted him to pray certain things over people or asked him to do certain things or go to certain places to fulfill a purpose.

But God had never asked him to say anything like this before!

The pastor tried to brush it off.

"Let's just wait on the Lord," he said to the family. "Let's wait for a word from the Lord."

Seconds had passed, but for the pastor it felt like minutes, or even hours. He couldn't shake the prompting in his spirit.

*It's just my own thoughts*, he thought, trying to convince himself. *God would never say something like this.*

He proceeded to pray a simple blessing over the food and the young woman's upcoming journey.

As everyone ate, laughed, and shared stories of their joyous times together with the Lord and the family, the pastor still couldn't shake the feeling that he hadn't done what God wanted him to do. He battled throughout the meal and hardly enjoyed the food or the company around the table.

When the meal had ended, just before everyone started to depart, the pastor announced that the Lord had a word for this young lady. Everyone was excited to hear what God would declare over her life before the missions trip.

Again the Pastor hesitated, hoping God would change His mind. The family was waiting with bated breath.

"God hates mommies and daddies," the pastor finally declared.

Everyone was shocked! The young woman's face turned pale as a ghost. She broke into tears and ran from the room. The rest of the family looked around in disbelief and even anger at the pastor's words.

The pastor sat on the couch quietly as everyone looked on in horror. However, all he sensed was a quiet resolve. He felt at peace over what he had said, what he felt God had laid on his heart to declare.

After what seemed like an eternity, the parents and the young woman emerged from the room, cradling each other with reddened eyes. They sat on the couch next to the pastor. You could have heard a pin drop in the deathly quiet. With broken hearts and trembling voices, the parents began to share what their daughter had just shockingly revealed to them.

' From as young as three years old, the girl could remember an uncle in the family who visited regularly and often babysat her. This uncle had been sexually molesting her every chance he got. When she was in his care, he would slip into her room at night and take advantage of her. It had started with cuddling, then touching and fondling, until it escalated to full molestation.

"Let's play a game," he would tell her. "It's called 'Mommies and Daddies.'" He used the ruse of a game to make her feel like the molestation was okay.

After much weeping and hugging and consoling, the family called the authorities and informed them of the abuse that had taken place over the years. The uncle was arrested, charged, and sent to jail for his crimes.

Then began the long journey of counselling and healing for the young woman, her parents, and the whole family. She did eventually go into the mission field full-time, but not until she'd gone through many hours of counselling and prayer.

The reason why I share this story is to remind people that many times it's not "stranger danger" we need to be aware of. Sadly, the danger can be posed by those around us, people who are close, including friends and family members. Sexual predators, pedophiles, and perpetrators use people's trust to make their advances. They use lies and deceit to ambush the young and vulnerable. They try to make their victim feel like their actions are normal.

But having someone touch you inappropriately in an unwanted way is never normal. It's never okay. Our privates are private for a reason. They're ours and ours alone.

Predators use gifts and bribes to get their way. When someone who's being abused lashes back or tries to deny their advances, a predator will often use threats of harm, perhaps even threatening the lives of someone in the family. They'll tell even more lies to fuel their sexual addiction.

If you or someone you know has been abused, or are being abused, please speak up. Be a voice for those who are unable to use their own voices. Someone may feel trapped and don't think they have any way out. Tell someone. Get help. Reach out to the authorities, a friend, or a loved one you can trust. If they don't listen, find someone else who will. You're not the bad guy. It's not your fault when you are sexually abused. You are a victim—but one day you can be victorious over the fear and shame of sexual abuse.

# 13

## The Journey Continues

MORE THAN A decade has passed since our world had been turned upside-down. Our lives have settled down as we raised our two miracle babies.

We still get occasional calls for help from Ericka and Jimmy, and we help whenever we can. But we can't always be there for them, since they've chosen their lifestyle and put themselves in their own desperate situations.

Focusing on our biological children has kept us going all these years—that and our faith and trust in God.

Johnny and Nate also reach out sometimes. They have both apologized and I believe they are coming to terms with what they did. We continue to pray for them and hope all the best for their futures. They are still young and have time so much potential.

As for Angel, we haven't heard from her, but we continue to hope that one day she will reach out to us.

Well, that's our story—so far.

We all strive for our final eternal destination, but we must not forget to enjoy the journey along the way. We have been through so much. Here we are at the end of the day, though, with our heads held high knowing that we are not bad parents. We did everything in our power to raise our children to the best of our ability, provide love and support, and bring them up in the love and admonition of the Lord.

God has been so good to us. His grace truly is sufficient.

Years ago, I heard a definition of grace that resonated with me. Grace gives you the ability to do what you cannot do. It gives you the ability to love the unlovable. It gives you the fortitude to go on even when you've been knocked down again and again. It gives you strength when you have none left. This is God's grace, His amazing grace.

For years we had prayed to have our own child. When it didn't happen, we just wanted to foster. We had so much love to give. We always got involved in children's and youth ministries at the churches we attended. And we ended up raising more than forty children, adopting two, and trying to adopt three others.

"Lord, it's okay if we don't have our own child," we prayed. "We will do our best to raise the children You have blessed us with."

Then, after nineteen years of marriage, we had Jewels. And a couple of years later, God gave us Josie. Knowing what we would go through, the Lord added to our lives through these precious biological children. They have added so much joy to our lives.

The arrival of our daughters was so timely. If we'd had children when we first got married at age twenty, we probably never would have fostered. God had a plan for us.

Annie always says that when life gives you lemons, make lemonade. Life can make you bitter, or it can make you better. Choose better. It's not what happens to you; it's what happens in you that's important at the end of the day.

How have you allowed the things that have happened to you affect you on the inside?

Yes, all of our children call, message, or stop by from time to time. It's painful to see them in difficult conditions, but we just must keep praying for and encouraging them when we get the chance. We love them.

With everything that's happened, our love for them will never grow cold or die. We know God's word to be true: *"Direct your children onto the right path, and when they are older, they will not leave it"* (Proverbs 22:6). We raised our children in the house of God and showed them who God is. Those things will never leave them. They will always be there. One day the Holy Spirit will draw them to the Father's heart. One day they will be restored and become the people of God He has called them to be.

One day, they will not only be our children but also children of God.

# Appendix

A FEW YEARS back, Annie took a course for which she studied FAS/FAE—in other words, fetal alcohol syndrome and fetal alcohol effects disorder. Of all the foster children we cared for, most likely they all had FAS/FAE to some extent. It is certain that Nate, Johnny, Angel, Ericka, and Jimmy all did.

When women drink during pregnancy, it affects their unborn child's development in the womb. Alcohol can do great damage, the effects of which we've seen firsthand. The boys did what they did because they were born damaged. We were their external consciences, since their internal consciences were compromised. If we were around, the boys behaved. When we weren't there, they were unable to make appropriate choices. They just didn't have the faculties. That's why Jimmy and Ericka chose drugs and alcohol and their friends over family. They didn't know how to make the right decisions.

The following informative article was written by Annie. If you know someone who's pregnant, please encourage them not to drink.

## FASD Is Not a Rapper

Fetal alcohol syndrome disorder, or fetal alcohol spectrum disorder, is a serious health problem that tragically affects its victims, their families, and peers, but it is completely preventable. Fetal alcohol syndrome is a condition characterized by abnormal features, growth retardation, and central nervous system problems. It can occur if a woman drinks alcohol during pregnancy.

## What Is FASD?

Fetal alcohol syndrome disorder is a highly variable group of birth defects, including mental retardation, deficient growth, and malformation of the skull and face. It tends to occur in the offspring of women who consume large amounts of alcohol during pregnancy.

Fetal alcohol syndrome disorder affects the brain, which leads to learning disabilities, behaviour problems, memory deficits, attention deficits, hyperactivity, or mental retardation. Someone with FASD may look normal on the outside, but their brain is damaged. The corpus callosum and frontal lobes are affected by alcohol exposure. In a normal brain, their behaviours are perceived to be inappropriate and immature.

The corpus callosum separates the right brain from the left brain. The left brain controls rules, consequences, concrete ideas, practical details, and orderly sequences. The right brain controls abstract thinking, emotions and feelings, creativity, and intuition. The corpus callosum helps both sides of the brain to work together.

In persons with FASD, the corpus callosum is damaged and cannot make the connection. Someone with FASD is not able to think before they act, even though they know the rules. It's like the brain has no brakes because of the damage that alcohol has done to the brain.

## Who Does FASD Affect?

FASD affects the person who has the disorder as well as their family, peers, classmates, colleagues, or anyone else they come into contact with. FASD can affect anyone regardless of ethnicity, income, or education level.

Every individual with FASD is different and what works for one may not work for another. To care for this person, you will need a plan that is based on their individual needs. Also it is best to get a diagnosis for FASD, because many resources are available to help individuals with FASD, whereas people without a diagnosis aren't eligible for those resources.

## Strategies

The following strategies can assist individuals with FASD:

1. Remember that brain damage is the basis for the challenging behaviour.
2. Try to change the environment rather than change the individual.
3. Visual, verbal, or symbolic cues can be used to remind the individual about tasks or behaviours. This can help counter their memory deficiency.
4. It's best to practice structure, boundaries, and consistency. Chaotic environments will lead to chaotic individuals. Boundaries are needed and consistency will help the individual with FASD. Structure for them a regular routine with simple rules and concrete one-step instructions.

5. Educate yourself and teach others what you learn. Also educate the individual about their disability. The more educated they are, the better they will be able to cope with their own challenges.

## Helping Adults and Teens with FASD

As a child with FASD grows into adulthood, they and their family face a whole new set of challenges. Because adults of FASD act in ways that are closer to those who are half their chronological age, they will need assistance to live successfully on their own.

Here are some steps to help.

1. Meet your child on their level. Just because they are an adult doesn't mean they no longer need your help and supervision. Attend appointments and/or interviews with them.
2. Engage your child in decision-making. Offer options for them to choose from, assist them in making decisions, and remind them that their choices affect themselves and others.
3. Involve others in your child's life, such as a friend, spouse, or roommate to help with job searches, cooking lessons, basic hygiene, money management, and wakeup calls.
4. Find a surrogate parent or guardian and train them to work with your child.
5. Help your child explain FASD to others. Knowledge is power.
6. Help your child manage their money. Set up a system so their bills get paid and groceries are bought.
7. Explore possible living arrangements, such as getting a roommate or living in an assisted living situation.

8. Connect your child with employment agencies for people with disabilities.

## Secondary Effects of FASD

The secondary effects include:

- mental health problems
- trouble in school
- trouble with the law
- confinement (incarceration or inpatient treatment for mental health problems or drug or alcohol abuse)
- inappropriate sexual behaviour
- substance abuse
- difficulty living on their own
- unemployment or difficulty keeping a job

Remember that these secondary effects are interconnected. They can arise all at once or develop one at a time depending on the situation.

For example, if your child is having trouble in school, they may start hanging with the wrong crowd and get involved with drugs. They can get into trouble with the law in their efforts to get money to pay for drugs.

Raising successful individuals with FASD means having a strong support system in place for them and being involved, watching out for warning signs of these secondary effects. If they appear, you need to get help as soon as possible. Remember that you are your child's best advocate.

## Medical Guidelines for Diagnosing FASD

There is no one test to diagnose FASD. Instead healthcare professionals look for the following signs and symptoms:

1. Abnormal facial features, such as a smooth ridge between the nose and upper lip (smooth philtrum), a thin upper lip, and a short distance between the inner and outer corners of the eyes, make their eyes seem widely spaced.
2. Growth problems such as low birth weight.
3. Central nervous system problems such as having trouble moving, speaking, or learning. They can also have problems with memory, senses, or social skills.
4. Mothers who use alcohol during pregnancy. It is unknown how much alcohol consumption is safe during pregnancy.

Other testing may also include MRIs, CT scans, and cognitive testing.

## Medicines

Many doctors with recognized expertise in FASD recommend that, in general, most kids with FASD do best with a combination of stimulant selective serotonin receptive inhibitors.

Medications that seem to be effective include Adderall, Ritalin, Concerta, or Dexedrine. Inhibitor drugs include Paxil, Prozac, Zoloft, and Celexa. These are the safest drugs with the least side effects. Some side effects include loss of appetite and an inability to sleep, so doctors sometimes prescribe Clonidine (Catapres).

Drugs don't cure FASD, but they can help the individual function and give them a better chance to succeed in life.

## Focussing on Prevention

Mothers and their partners need to make healthy choices prior to pregnancy. No amount of alcohol is safe during pregnancy. A parent would never give a baby a bottle full of alcohol, so expectant mothers need to consider the actions they take while carrying an unborn child. Education and awareness are the best teachers.

In many provinces in Canada, many licensed bars and restaurants and stores that sell alcohol must now post signs warning women about the risks of drinking during pregnancy. The signs are prominently displayed.

## Conclusion

FASD is often known as an invisible diagnosis, in that many people go undiagnosed because of a lack of knowledge of the syndrome. People need to know that FASD is real and preventable. Education and awareness are key. If you are pregnant or know someone who is pregnant, make sure to let them know the dangers of drinking during pregnancy.

## About the Author

EDDIE KAT IS originally from Newfoundland. He moved north to the James Bay area in 1989 to work for the Hudson's Bay Company. There, he met the love of his life, Annie. After a year of dating, they decided to elope to Winnipeg, Manitoba.

Married at the tender age of twenty, they quickly discovered that they couldn't have children of their own. Because they loved children and wanted to have a family, they began to foster children.

They fostered and raised more than forty children, adopted two, and tried to adopt three others. After nineteen years of marriage and many years of prayer, God then blessed them with two miracle children of their own.

After more than three decades of marriage, Eddie is ready to share his journey of heartbreak, healing, and hope.